PRINTED AND PUBLISHED IN GREAT BRITAIN BY D.C. THOMSON & CO. LTD., 185 FLEET STREET, LONDON EC4A 2HS.
© D.C. THOMSON & CO. LTD., 1990.
ISBN 0-85116-481-1

TOPPER '53

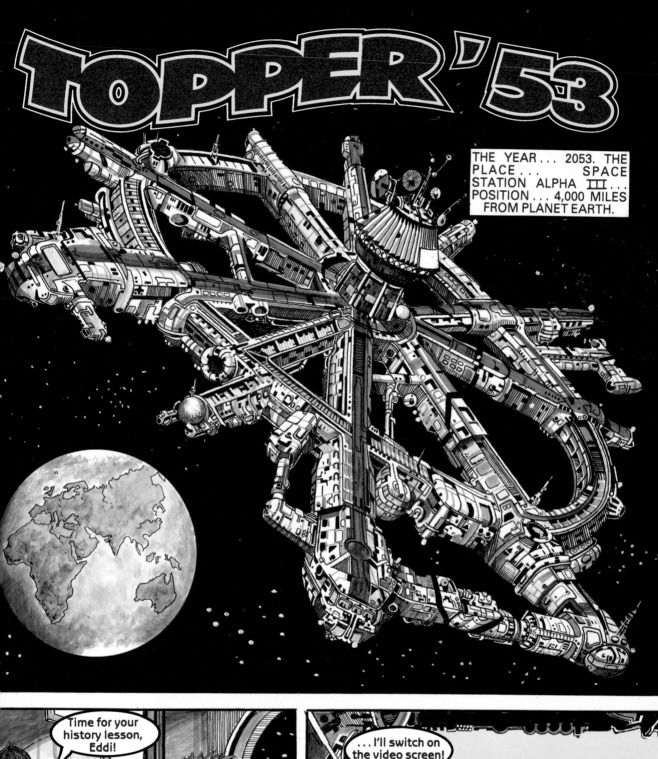

THE YEAR... 2053. THE PLACE... SPACE STATION ALPHA III... POSITION... 4,000 MILES FROM PLANET EARTH.

Time for your history lesson, Eddi!

Data accepted, Mum...

...I'll switch on the video screen!

100 YEARS AGO

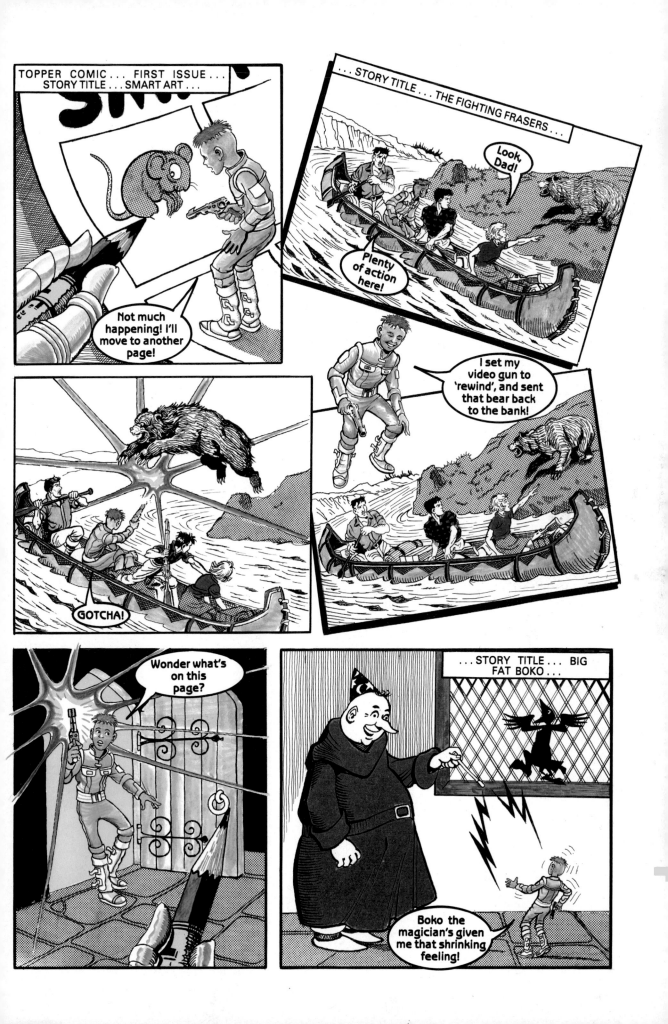

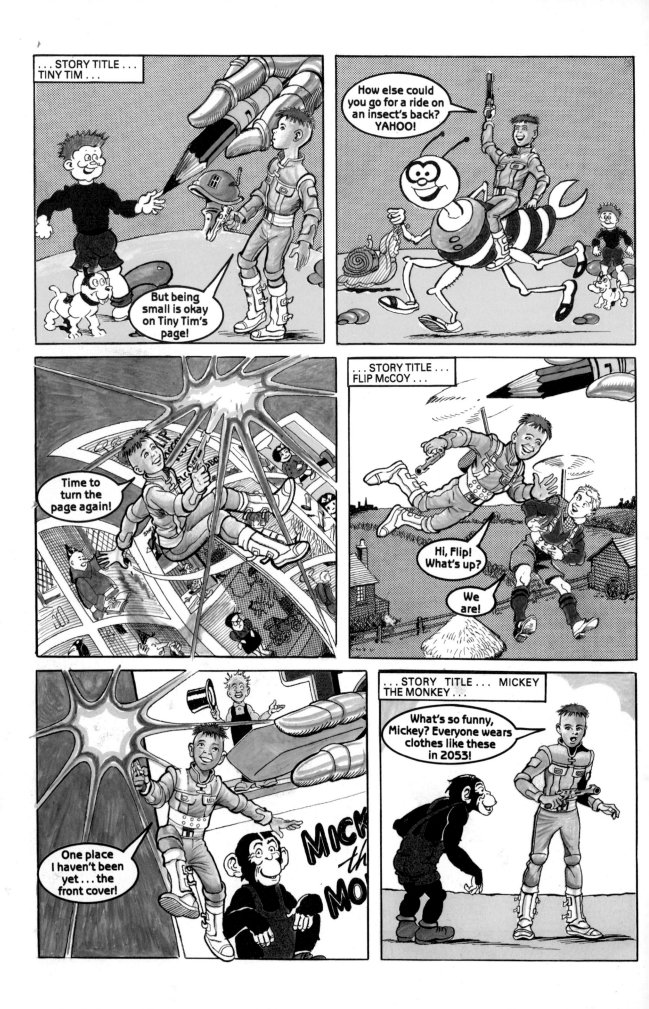

F